SIX WORD
LESSONS

FOR
SUCCESSFUL
TRIATHLETES

100 Lessons

for

Essential Training

and Racing

Lance Carter

Six-Word Lessons for Successful Triathletes

Published by Pacelli Publishing
9905 Lake Washington Blvd. NE, #D-103
Bellevue, Washington 98004
PacelliPublishing.com

ISBN-10: 1-933750-50-2
ISBN-13: 978-1-933750-50-7

Introduction

My mission and purpose in life is to inspire people to live more fulfilling lives through exercise and mindset elevation. Coaching triathletes allows me to live my purpose on a daily basis and for that I am grateful! Nearly every one of us can raise our self-esteem and confidence, helping us to go after our bigger dreams. Mindset elevation is precisely why the last chapter of this book is titled, Applying Lessons of Triathlon to Life.

I love using triathlon as a vehicle for boosting self-esteem, confidence, and mindset of the athletes I coach. I'm so excited to be putting out this book so I can reach more athletes with my triathlon lessons.

In writing this book, two big life lessons have been reinforced for me - taking bold action, and allowing myself to show vulnerability. The first few times I told people I was writing a book, it felt empowering and terrifying at the same time. It's a bold thing to announce that you are going to write a book. By allowing myself to be vulnerable I have received some invaluable advice. I've shared my book with a few people, risking feeling and looking like a fool if they thought what I had written was complete crap. This allowed me to receive some very helpful feedback. In fact, this book probably never would have happened if

Karra Whitmire of Sub 3 Life Coaching had not recommended that I speak with Patty at Pacelli Publishing. I had posted on my Facebook page that I was writing a book and was trying to figure out how to get my book published. I tracked down several leads, but it was Karra's tip that led me to Patty. Acting with boldness and vulnerability has paid off with a published book!

The same attitude is required in triathlon. It's very bold to embark on your first triathlon, or a longer distance triathlon for the first time. Admitting that you need help, or that you are nervous or scared takes courage and the risk of vulnerability. However, when you allow yourself to take those risks you emerge as a stronger person. It is my greatest hope that through the sport of triathlon you discover new inner strength that propels you to further greatness in your daily life. Wishing you all the best in your triathlon endeavors!

Acknowledgements

In my 23 years training and racing in the sport of triathlon, I have tried to absorb as much information as I could on training methodology. I have, of course, made and learned from lots of mistakes of my own along the way. There is one person however, from whom I've learned more from than any other. As a coach for Team In Training (TNT) for 17 years, I was fortunate that for many of those years Dave Scott, six-time Ironman Champion, was the National Head Coach. Dave did coaching certification programs for "chapter coaches" of TNT.

I was incredibly lucky to attend both Level I and II certifications. Imagine being in a room with Dave and about 16 other coaches for nearly three days and over eight hours a day. I can't even tell you how geeked out I was. In addition, Dave was at several of the races that I was coaching with TNT and I was able to listen to him speak to our athletes on many occasions.

The biggest thing that surprised me, and something I've tried to model, was how interested Dave was in us. I remember at the Level I clinic he said, "No one cares how much you know, until they know how much you care." I found out 17 years later that it was Theodore Roosevelt who said that, but I've been crediting Dave with that quote since I heard it. Either way, it made me a better coach. I would highly encourage you to subscribe to Dave's newsletter at *DaveScottInc.com*. I can't tell you the number of excellent tips I've picked up over the years.

Dedication

This book is dedicated to the thousands of athletes I've coached over the past 20-plus years, many of whom I've coached through Team In Training. GO TEAM! I'm grateful for all the friendships that have been created along the way. And to my nephew, Geddy Brunson, stay strong in your fight against Leukemia. Eleven years from now when you are 18, I hereby challenge you to a race at the Lavaman Triathlon where we can be a part of Team In Training together.

Kris and Ted

It's been so great coaching you both.

Can't wait for IM Wisconsin.

Lance

Table of Contents

General Training Principles to Guide You

1

Dude, don't take yourself so seriously.

Odds are you're not going to become a professional triathlete. Don't make your training and racing so critical that you forsake your family and friends because you "need to train." Find the balance. Triathlon should be a part of and enhance your life; it needn't become your entire life.

2

Engage in your training with seriousness.

By all means, treat your training seriously. Train with intention and purpose. That is completely different from making it your entire life. Triathlon will add a whole host of benefits to the enjoyment of your life. When you are training, be fully engaged in the moment. Be present in training and in life.

3

Too much, too soon equals injury.

It's common when you begin a new training program to be excited and want to do more. Your body needs time to adapt to the new levels and forms of stress. Be consistent but take it slow. Don't overdo it. Give your body time to adapt. Don't do too much too soon.

4

Reasons to keep a training log

Recording your training creates a system of accountability for yourself. When you know you're going to have to confess to your training log that you skipped your workout, it's a powerful motivator. Training logs can help you uncover hidden information should you experience injury. They can also help you plan future training based on past performance.

5

You can create your own motivation.

Every person who trains for a triathlon will eventually have times when motivation wanes. Just knowing that fact will help you understand it's "not just you" and that you are not alone or "weak." Defining your training and racing goals will create motivation. Training partners and group workouts are excellent ways to create motivation as well.

6

Train to race, race to train.

Having a race on your calendar just far enough into the future is an excellent way to motivate yourself. Talk to other triathletes and you will find out how common this strategy is. You will also learn that others struggle with finding ways to motivate themselves. It's much easier to skip workouts without a race on the horizon.

7

Understand WHY you are doing this.

Write down all the reasons why you are doing triathlon. What do you want to accomplish? How will training and racing benefit your life in aspects beyond the sport? Will it help you create a support network and friends? Will it help you boost your confidence? Anytime you find yourself needing motivation, read your list of reasons.

8

A training plan is your roadmap.

Make sure you have a training plan. There are many available for purchase, for free on the internet, or you can hire a triathlon coach to create a training plan for you. A plan will give your training the structure it needs and it will help lead you toward your race goals. In essence, it simplifies your training.

9

It's the work, not the plan.

Having a training plan is important for sure. However, it's the work, the actual training, which leads to results. Too many people spend too much time searching for the perfect plan before they begin any actual training. The magic is in the work, not the plan. The best training plan is the one you do.

10

Stick to the schedule, allowing flexibility.

It's important to follow your training plan while at the same time allowing for flexibility and adjustment. Life happens. Weather happens. Injuries happen. If you have a long bike ride scheduled for Saturday and a long run scheduled for Sunday and the weather calls for rain Saturday but not Sunday, it might be more enjoyable to swap your workouts.

11

Utilizing the principle of progressive overload

Increase the work load consistently and gradually. The body needs time to adapt but once it does, a new greater stimulus needs to be applied for further progress. Training programs consistently and gradually add longer workouts over a period of weeks and months. Doing the same workout at the same effort continually will not lead to progress.

12

Consistency, the key ingredient to improvement

"The number one most important rule of training, which is often forgotten, is consistency. There is no training program or workout any coach can devise that can make up for a lack of consistency in training." -Jim Vance, CoachVance.com. Amen, Jim! Couldn't have said it better myself.

13

Every workout should have a purpose.

Understanding the purpose of the workout before you begin is important. Each workout is a piece of the puzzle that works in harmony with the other workouts in your training plan. Is the purpose of a particular workout to build strength? Speed? Endurance? Promote recovery? Maintain fitness? Eliminate "junk" mileage. Train with a purpose. Train with intention.

14

Learn to listen to your body.

Listening to your body is the invaluable skill needed to keep aches and pains from becoming injuries. Missing workouts due to injury directly undermines the importance of consistency. Learn to recognize and address when a muscle, tendon, or joint is strained or sore and treat it. Too many people ignore the signs hoping they will magically disappear, then they get injured.

15

Take planned rest or forced rest.

You'll either take planned rest periods, making adjustments needed to allow your body to recover and repair itself, or you will ignore your body only to have it force you to take a break due to injury. The choice is yours. Planned breaks are much shorter than forced breaks. Better to miss a day than a week.

16

Recovery is critical to promoting growth.

Your body needs increased stimulus and it needs rest and recovery. When it comes to recovery your main objective is to increase blood flow while minimizing muscular tension. Oxygen and nutrients needed for tissue repair are delivered via the bloodstream, which is why increasing blood flow is important. Think swimming, aqua jogging, and high cadence plus low resistance cycling.

17

Incorporate self-care into your weekly routine.

When you stress your muscles and tendons through training you also need to allow your body to recover so it can grow stronger. You can speed the recovery process up through a variety of techniques including, but not limited to: massage, self-massage, (foam rollers, "The Stick") stretching, yoga, ice baths, and core strengthening.

18

Alternate easy days with hard days.

Your weekly training should have an ebb and flow to it such that you alternate easier days with harder days. For example, a swim workout the day following a hard run workout will help your legs recover from the previous day's run. The recovery will prepare them for another harder workout on the bike or run the day following the swim.

19

Every third or fourth week - recover.

As you progress week to week through your training, periodically allow your body to recover more deeply. Schedule an "easy week" where you swim more, bike with light pedal resistance, and run in the water. It's common to have every third or fourth week be a recovery week. Reduce your training volume. It's also an opportunity to work on skill development.

20

Road ID - get it, wear it.

Visit RoadID.com and buy yourself an easy to wear identification tag or bracelet. Training for a triathlon comes with certain risks, especially but not limited to sharing the roads with cars, so accidents can happen. Make sure that if you are injured in an accident your training partners or other people have your name and emergency contact information.

21

Keep your blood iron levels up.

It's not uncommon for triathletes to find themselves periodically feeling more tired than normal. Should you experience this, have your iron levels checked. At the very least, try boosting your iron levels with some liquid iron and through food sources high in iron such as spinach, kale, chick peas, red meat, and liver.

22

A brief introduction to Perceived Exertion.

It is very helpful if you learn to rate your level of exertion in training. Perceived Exertion (PE) is an extremely useful tool when racing. One of the most common mistakes in racing is going out too fast. Monitoring your PE throughout the race, especially the first half, can keep you from making this mistake.

23

You cannot cram for your triathlon.

The physical adaptations your body needs to make in order to prepare you for your race take weeks and months. Training for a triathlon is not like studying for a test in school - you cannot cram for it at the last minute. Give your body's muscles and tendons the time they need to adapt to the training.

24

Brick workouts, a staple of triathlons

The most common brick workout is a bike followed by a run. Every triathlete can recall the first time they tried to run after cycling. There's an unusual feeling in the legs to say the least, but with practice the transition from biking to running gets easier to deal with. Combining workouts is an excellent way to train with specificity.

25

Want to be fast?
Be lean.

What do pro triathletes have in common? They are all lean. The same holds true if you look at the winners of your age group. In addition to working out, you need to eat a clean diet with lots of high quality foods. Being leaner makes it easier and faster to run and bike, especially when your bike is headed uphill.

26

Strength training your core and glutes

Any physical therapist will tell you how important it is to strengthen your core, which is much more than "six-pack abs." Your glutes are vital to maintaining proper body position all the way through the running gait cycle. According to physical therapists, weak and inactive glutes are at the root of many running injuries.

Swim – Become One with the Water

27

Hire a swim coach for technique.

Especially if you are new to swimming, invest in some swim coaching for yourself. Anyone swimming slower than 1:30 per 100 yards can certainly benefit from improving their technique. One single coached lesson can accelerate your swimming improvement by weeks. A better swim split in a race will help you conserve energy for the bike and run.

28

Focus more on technique than effort.

Swimming well is about efficiency. Beginning swimmers, especially athletes who are experienced in cycling and running, often think they can simply try harder and they'll swim faster. While this works in cycling and running, trying harder in swimming does not work. Because technique in swimming is critical, focus on form over effort.

29

Train like a swim team swimmer.

Swimmers work out with lots of intervals and predetermined rest periods between reps. Many triathletes, especially beginners, tend to swim continuously without pausing for a certain times or distances. This creates slow swimmers. Doing structured swim workouts will not only make the time go by faster, it will make the workouts more enjoyable, and create faster swimmers.

30

Learn to use a swim clock.

A key component in structured swim workouts is using a swim clock. Use it to time your work intervals and to monitor your rest periods between reps and sets. Use it to learn your average 100 pace. Knowing your average 100 pace will allow you to gauge your progress. Improvement in form will show up with faster swim times.

31

Swimming is your best recovery workout.

Scheduling a swim workout following a hard bike ride or hard run workout is an incredibly effective training strategy. Because biking and running primarily fatigue your legs and swimming is primarily an upper body sport, swimming promotes increased blood flow to your legs without causing further muscle fatigue.

32

Wetsuit shorts improve your body position.

Ideally you'll learn to swim with a balanced body position and do so without the use of swim aides. That being said, wetsuit shorts instantly correct poor body position and allow you to focus on improving your swim stroke. Learning proper exhalation and correct body position are two of the most common challenges for new swimmers.

33

Open water swim training, think safety

It's safer to swim with a partner in open water than to swim alone. The safety buoy/dry bags are pure genius! Get yourself one. Wear a brightly colored swim cap for increased visibility. As much as possible, choose bodies of water free of boats and jet skis, etc.

34

Make sure to practice your sighting.

Most triathletes have a story about veering way off course in one of their first races. Avoid this mistake by practicing your sighting every time you swim in open water. Sight every ten to twenty strokes. In training you won't have buoys to sight on but you can choose any landmark in the distance to sight on.

35

The sun as a navigational tool

Sometimes the sun is shining directly at you in a blinding manner. If you figure out where you need to keep the sun in your field of vision you can use it to make sure you are swimming straight. If it's squarely in your left eye and then it's moved off to your right eye, you have veered to the left.

36

Learn to breathe on both sides.

If the sun is blinding you on one side and your vision is compromised you can switch to breathing on the opposite side. The same holds true if the water is choppy and the waves are coming from one side. Breathing to the opposite side will allow you to take a breath without getting a mouthful of water.

37

Preview swim course at race time.

Preview the swim course at the same time as the race. Notice the position of the sun and determine if it's going to cause you sighting issues. Use this practice swim to identify notable landmarks that will help with your sighting. Are there any tall buildings or unusual tress that stand out and that you can use to your advantage?

38

For your race, seed yourself accordingly.

If it's your first race or you are anxious for the swim, begin at the back and to the outside of the group. This keeps you out of the fray. You want your race to get off to a good start and not get pummeled. If you are a fast swimmer, go to the front of the pack.

39

Be cautious at the turn buoys.

Other than the start of a triathlon swim, the turn buoys are the most chaotic and dangerous spots on a swim course. If you are nervous about the swim it would be better to take a slightly wider path around the buoys so you can have more "clear" water and avoid contact from other swimmers as much as possible.

40

Swim in - far as you can.

When finishing the swim in the race, swim in to shore until your hand touches the bottom and then take another shallow stroke or two. This way you pop up in ankle deep water as opposed to putting your feet down as soon as possible, then having to attempt to run through waist-deep water.

Bike – Roughly 50% of Your Race

41

Work on your bike handling skills.

Spend some time specifically working on skills such as cornering, climbing, descending, standing, accelerating, braking, cadence, controlling the bike with one hand, engaging your core, creating a smooth pedal stroke, riding in the aero position and being able to look around you and still ride straight. Check your local bike shop for classes.

42

A professional bike fit is beneficial.

You'll be more comfortable if you are professionally fit on your bike. There are a myriad of changes that can be made so that your bike fits your anatomy, which will result in a more comfortable ride. You'll also be able to generate more power resulting in a faster ride. Make sure you begin with a bike that is your size.

43

Aerobars will simply make you faster.

Riding in the aero position will reduce drag resulting in riding faster. This requires a different bike fit than a road position. Riding in the aero position will result in one of your biggest time gains during your triathlon. Make sure you are comfortable in this position and that you practice riding in it.

44

Bright lights might save your life.

Ride with rechargeable front and rear lights, even in the day. Everyone should be riding with them. They are very powerful, extra bright, small, and easy to install. Riding on the roads is one of the most dangerous things you'll do as a triathlete so make sure you do all you can to live to train another day.

45

Race course specificity - train with purpose.

Bike courses vary wildly from race to race; make sure you practice on course conditions and profiles similar to your race. Does your race have steep hills? Tight corners? Long straight flat stretches where you'll need to be in the aero position for long periods of time? Find out and create training routes that mimic the race course.

46

Bike faster in training than racing.

Spend time training faster than you anticipate biking during your race. Too often triathletes ride harder during a race than they do in training which causes them to have a disastrous run split. Spend time riding harder in training than the projected race pace/effort. This way you can save a little during the bike and have an excellent run.

47

Cadence helps you learn to shift.

If your cadence drops below your target, shift to an easier gear. If your cadence rises above your target, shift to a harder (faster) gear. Shifting gears properly and with good timing is one of the more challenging bike skills for beginners; using cadence can help you learn proper timing. There's no one ideal cadence, but 85 to 95 is common.

48

Read the road ahead of you.

Scan the road ahead of you for clues on how you will adjust your approach. Does the road rise ahead or descend? How steeply and for how long? Are there curves coming up and how sharp are they? Are there pot holes or other obstacles you need to avoid? How will you adjust your body weight and shift gears to compensate?

49

Your eyes can guide your bike.

Your bike goes where you focus your eyes. Focus to the side of an obstacle, like a pothole, instead of on it. Focus your gaze up the road rather than three feet in front of your bike in order to ride steadier. In a corner, focus beyond the turn to get your bike to go in the direction you want.

50

Engage your core, maintain "light hands."

Keep your core engaged so that your hands rest lightly on the handle bars or your elbows rest lightly on the aerobar pads. Your fingers should be relaxed as if you could play the piano and not have a death grip on the bars. Engaging your core keeps your upper bodyweight from slumping on to the bars.

51

Steering your bike with your weight.

You do more steering of your bike with pressure from your hands and shifting your body weight than actual turning of the handle bars. As you ride try adding more pressure to one hand than the other and notice where your bike steers. When navigating turns try opening up your inside knee and notice how your bike reacts.

52

Learn to change
a flat tire.

While learning to change a flat tire is intimidating to new cyclists, it's really not very hard. Stop by your local bike shop and ask them if they provide flat tire changing classes or ask them to show you how to change a flat tire. And there is always YouTube.

53

Do some quick basic bike maintenance.

Taking 60 seconds to wipe down your bike after your ride is a fantastic habit to develop. Keep your chain cleaned and lubed on a regular basis. Check your chain periodically for excessive wear and replace it before it gets over-stretched. Check your tires for cuts and embedded debris. Make sure your brake pads are not worn and are aligned properly.

54

Taking a bottle on the fly.

One skill you need to learn is grabbing a water bottle while cycling. When using aid stations on the bike course you'll want to continue riding while grabbing a water bottle and placing it the bottle cage. For beginning and intermediate triathletes this is a skill that needs to be practiced, especially at 18-22 mph.

Run – One Step at a Time

55

Your form matters, run more efficiently.

Running efficiently will make running easier on your body, make running feel like less effort, and allow you to run faster. Running efficiently is about running with proper running form. Keeping a cadence of 180 steps per minute or higher is an excellent starting point for running with "Best Form."

56

Strangely, your arms control your legs.

If you want to increase your cadence, speed up your arm cadence. If your hands and arms are extending beyond your torso too much it will cause your legs to reach forward and cause you to over-stride resulting in heel striking. If your hands are low it will cause a slow leg turnover.

57

Train at a variety of intensities.

Mix up your training intensity, pace and effort. The majority of your running should be at an Easy to Moderate effort (aerobic training), but not all of it. Include some higher intensity running (anaerobic training). Do speed work in the Hard to Very Hard range and tempo work in the Moderately Hard to Hard range.

58

Your aerobic pace equals conversational pace.

Since the majority of your running should be in your aerobic training zone, an easy way to make sure that you are in this zone is to maintain a steady unbroken conversation. If you are running alone (and no one is around, so you don't appear crazy) simply begin talking as a test. If you can't, then slow down.

59

Use training groups to your advantage.

Group runs often turn into speed workouts given the competitive nature of athletes. This is fine if you intend on using the group for your speed workout, but not if your goal is an easy run. Know the purpose of your workout so that you can use training groups to your advantage.

60

Do a pre-run dynamic warmup routine.

Prepare for your runs with a quick 5 to 10-minute dynamic warmup routine. Give your muscles a chance to warm up and elongate before putting them under the stress load that running demands. There are several routines just an internet search away. Give it a try and notice how much better you feel when you begin your run.

61

Running in colder climates, use layers.

Dress in layers if you run in colder climates. This allows you to shed layers as you heat up. Jackets, long sleeve shirts, and vests can be tied around your waist. Gloves and head bands can be tucked into your waistband. The more you run and take note of the temperatures, the more you will dial in your running wardrobe.

62

Dress for the 10-minute mark.

Since most people warm up quickly, plan your wardrobe for 10 minutes into your run. You may be just a little cold to begin with, but you'll be comfortable for the remainder of your run without carrying excess clothing tied around your waist. If you want to get blood flowing through your upper body prior to running, do some pushups.

63

If motivation to run is low . . .

. . . just run for 15 minutes. If after 15 minutes you still don't feel like running, then call it a day. Typically you will begin to feel better within 10 minutes and you'll decide that you want to keep going. Starting is often the hardest part. Make a deal with yourself to begin before deciding to cancel a run.

64

Learn to run off the bike.

Since your triathlon running occurs after biking, make sure you practice running after cycling. Your legs will typically feel heavy despite the fact that you are commonly running faster than you think. The more you practice, the easier the transition from cycling to running becomes. Take shorter, quicker steps to begin, which allows you to settle into a rhythm.

65

Run in water for recovery/injury.

Deep water running is an excellent recovery workout as well as one of the best workouts to replace a run if you are dealing with an injury. Even speed workouts can be done in the water, allowing you to maintain your fitness. For long runs and runs at an Easy to Moderate effort, runners commonly use a flotation belt.

66

Change it up now and then.

Mix up your running; don't get stuck running the same route in the same direction, in the same pair of shoes, at the same time of day, etc. Try some trail running. Alternate your shoes; lighter shoes can be helpful for speed workouts and a shoe with more midsole can be helpful for longer runs.

Transitions – The Fourth Sport of Triathlon

67

Transitions: the fourth component of triathlons

Transitioning from the swim to the bike and from the bike to the run requires practice, just as swimming, biking, and running do. Make sure that you practice setting up your transition area and do some run-throughs so you can not only gain experience, but learn to make them more efficient and smooth.

68

Keep it simple, keep it uncluttered.

Take only your necessities into your transition area. Extra "stuff" only clutters your area, makes your process less streamlined, and slows you down. Your goal should be to quickly and smoothly get out of the transition area. The more organized and simple your transition is laid out the better.

69

Know the ins and the outs.

Every transition area has a "Swim In," "Bike Out," "Bike In," and "Run Out" location. Make sure you know where they are located before the race begins. Do not rely on the volunteers; it's your responsibility to not only know where they are located but to know your path to and from your bike rack location.

70

Conduct a pre-race walkthrough of transition.

Prior to race start, walk from where the swim exits the water to the "Swim In" area of transition. Review and commit to memory the location of your bike rack. Walk to the "Bike Out" location. Review the route from "Bike In" and the "Run Out" location. Doing this routine will save you lots of confusion and time during the race.

71

Count the number of bike racks.

From the "Swim In" area, memorize the number of bike racks to get to your row. For example, "5 rows, left turn, half way down." In the race, count the racks, turn into the correct row and go to your bike. Should you choose the wrong row and spend several minutes looking for your bike, you will appreciate this lesson!

72

The mount and dismount bike line

There is a line outside of transition, manned by volunteers called the Mount/Dismount Line. It's the line where you can officially mount your bike and not before. It's also the place where you must dismount your bike before entering transition. It's helpful to review the location of this line to your pre-race walkthrough even though it's pretty obvious during the race.

73

It's a very small dressing room.

Your "dressing room" in transition is quite small. It's about the width of a hand towel. Your handle bars can be often touching the handle bars of the bike next to you. Your space is roughly from your tire to the edge of your handle bars. This is why your transition needs to be tidy and organized without extra stuff.

74

Learn to run with your bike.

There is usually a short run with your bike required when exiting and entering the transition during the race. Learn to run alongside your bike. If you plan to put your shoes on before mounting your bike (as opposed to having your shoes clipped in to your pedals) you'll want to practice running in your bike shoes too.

75

Practice mounting and dismounting your bike.

Some methods of mounting and dismounting your bike are faster than others. The fastest methods require practice. Some people get on and off with their shoes still clipped into the pedals. Others get a running start wearing bike shoes and some go from a standstill. Whichever method you choose, make sure you practice it until you have it down.

76

What's a race number belt for?

The race number belt is an elastic band that clips around your waist to display your race number during the run. Simply click the belt with race bib attached in place as you exit for the run. Some races may still require you to wear your number on the bike but it's not as common since the introduction of bike numbers.

77

Make a transition checklist for yourself

Create your own, download one, or use an app for your transition checklist. This makes it convenient to pack for your race and to ensure you don't forget any of the necessary items. Create one using a spreadsheet and make two boxes to check off for each item, one to pack for the trip and one for the race.

78

Stop wasting time tying your shoes.

Put elastic laces in your running shoes or use cord locks on your traditional laces. Either way, quit tying your shoes! Since one of your goals should be to get out of transition as quickly as possible, eliminate the time consuming task of tying your shoes. You want your bike-to-run transition to be as smooth as possible, so eliminate unneeded tasks.

79

To sock or not to sock

Some triathletes are adamant about NOT wearing socks for the sake of speed. Some are equally adamant about not wanting to increase the chance of getting blisters. Whichever method you choose, just make sure to practice. Don't make the mistake of training with socks and then racing without socks when you haven't tested it out.

Racing – Move Through and Beyond Obstacles

80

Practice race morning breakfast in advance.

Practice eating the same breakfast before several training workouts that you will eat on the race morning. Think about the timing as well. How far in advance do you eat to allow for digestion? If you will be staying in a hotel without a kitchen on race morning, what type of food will you have access to? Practice with that food.

81

Practice race nutrition plan in advance.

Long workouts are excellent opportunities to practice your race nutrition plan. What type of food and drink do you prefer when exercising? Which nutrition works best with your digestive system? How many ounces of water or sports drink will you consume each hour? How many calories will you consume each hour? Where will those calories come from?

82

Dehydration creates a decrease in performance.

For endurance athletes, performance is impaired when dehydration results in a drop in as little as two percent of body weight. Make sure that you stay hydrated and make it a habit to drink the appropriate number of ounces of water or sports drink every hour while exercising. That number can vary by body weight, temperature, humidity, and exercise intensity.

83

Ice, oh it feels so good.

When racing in hot and humid environments, take advantage of ice at the run aid stations. Put it in your hat, down your shorts, in your top, and/or hold it in your hands. Ice helps cool your core body temperature. Plus, it improves your mood and helps you maintain a positive mental attitude which is required for optimal performance.

84

Split your race into manageable sections.

The longer the race, the more important it is to split the race into smaller manageable chunks of time and/or distance. This keeps the brain from becoming overwhelmed, helping you maintain a positive mental state. Focusing on a smaller chunk keeps you in the moment so you can concentrate on what needs your attention in that moment.

85

Excellent advice from "The Man" himself

Some of the best advice I've ever heard was from Dave Scott, six-time Ironman Champion known as "The Man." (DaveScottInc.com) On multiple occasions Dave Scott has given the following advice, "Do what you can do in the moment." Races will test your resolve and things will get hard; just focus on what you can do right then in that moment.

86

Prepare for things to go wrong.

You should visualize yourself having your optimal race, but also be prepared for things to go wrong and plan for overcoming these obstacles. Sometimes you get tangled up in the swim with a hand or foot and your goggles come off. Flat tires happen. Blisters happen. Things can go awry, but it's how you respond that makes the biggest difference.

87

Nothing new on your race day.

It's always best to race with equipment that you've used in training. This allows you to make needed adjustments prior to the race. It's best to practice with a particular brand of nutrition in training before racing. Find out what nutrition the race is serving on course and test it in training so you will know if you like it.

88

Thank a volunteer during the race.

If you've ever volunteered for a race you know what a thankless job it is. When you say, "Thank You," not only will it make the volunteer feel good, it will also boost your spirits. This will help put you and/or keep you in a positive mental state which elevates performance. It's simple, easy to do, and it works!

89

Know what you are grateful for.

Whenever things in the race get extra tough and you want to throw in the towel, think of something you are truly grateful for. When you do, you'll feel this incredible sense of power build deep within you. It will lift you out of your temporary place of pain and into a state of inspiration.

Applying Lessons of Triathlon to Life

90

Using triathlons to boost your confidence.

Whenever a person completes an event that they thought they couldn't, there is an increase in confidence. Initially the boost in confidence may just be for that particular accomplishment, but confidence in one area can and will increase confidence in self. This boost of self-confidence will allow you to tackle other new endeavors.

91

Create your daily routine for success.

Build daily and weekly habits and routines which lead to a productive healthy lifestyle. "We first make our habits, then our habits make us," said John Dryden. Consider your life for a moment. You are who you are because of what you do and think on a daily basis. If you want to change your life, change your habits.

92

It's okay to celebrate your accomplishments.

Make a daily habit of writing down the things that you did well each day. By doing this you will reinforce your self-confidence and acknowledge your competence. We beat ourselves up to the point that we have low self-esteem which creates ripple effects throughout our lives. When we celebrate our accomplishments we create ripple effects of the positive order.

93

For every negative thought, two positives

This strategy works wonders in racing and in life. Why is it so easy for us to subject ourselves to negative thoughts? Make a habit of replacing every negative thought with two positive ones. You'll be shocked to realize how often your mind goes negative. With this habit you'll be bombarding your mind with positivity and your mindset will shift.

94

Can you ask a better question?

Whenever you are overwhelmed or in a negative state of mind, utilize the power of questions to redirect your focus, which will open your mind to new possibilities. Ask yourself open ended questions, such as "What if . . .?" and allow your mind to come up with creative means to fulfill your request. Shift your focus toward possibility and away from doubt.

95

Focus on effort, opposed to results.

Focus on the effort and the results will take care of themselves. This is true in triathlon and it's true in life. Too often we focus on the result we want, but we ignore or are not complete in our efforts and our preparation. When we are fully prepared for our challenges, we get and often exceed our expected outcomes.

96

The competence/ confidence loop and you

Google the Competence/Confidence Loop. Boiled down it says: If you want to elevate your confidence in any area, increase your competence in that area. When you do, your confidence will grow which will encourage you to tackle bigger challenges in that area. Your competence grows again which boosts your confidence, and so on and so on.

97

Replace "have to" with "get to."

Notice how common it is for people to use the words "I have to," as in, "I have to work out today." "I have to go to work today." Take away that person's health or means for making an income and they'll be wishing they could exercise or go to work. This simple change will shift your mindset.

98

Go farther, go faster, challenge yourself.

When you complete a triathlon there's a natural inclination to ask yourself if you could go faster and/or complete a longer race. Go for it. Challenge yourself! Challenge yourself in sport and in life. You're going to feel most fulfilled when you are challenging yourself and pushing your comfort boundaries. Always being comfortable leads to complacency and boredom.

99

Elevate your mindset, elevate your life.

Allow yourself to consider the possibility that you are capable of accomplishing more in your life. Begin to shift your mindset from limitation and low self-esteem to a higher level. You will notice a shift in your thoughts and your energy. You will see the world differently and you will put yourself in a position to positively impact your own life.

100

Take action and change your life.

You must take action to positively impact your life. You must do it immediately and do it daily. By making decisions and taking action on these decisions you will be building a stronger circuitry within yourself which will allow you to go after your greatest dreams. You have a choice every day about the future of your life. Go for it!

Free Resources

I've created several free resources just for you! Simply go to a special page on my website that was created for you at **LanceCarterCoaching.com/LEARN**

On the web page I'm sharing several of my 10-minute strength training routines that came about from being sidelined for nine months and in physical therapy for triathlon related injuries.

In 2013, shortly after finishing Kona, I was extra-inspired to take my training to a new level and began running six days a week with an eye on a sub-3-hour marathon. Several months of this led to a severe foot injury. Doing my physical therapy incorrectly (completely my fault, not the PT's) created a hip injury on my opposite side. I was under the care of a couple of PT's for about 9 months. Not feeling like I had 30 minutes, 2 to 3 times a week, I decided to create 10-minute routines that incorporated the variety of PT exercises. Ten minutes was the least amount of time that I felt I could spare every day without any excuses. I've been doing my 10 minutes of PT strength training almost every day ever since and I can't believe how much stronger I feel. My friends have grown tired of me constantly telling them how great I feel.

It is required that you get approval from a medical professional before beginning any of the workouts and consult a fitness professional on the proper mechanics of the routines and movements.

Additionally, I am including several recordings of my weekly live coaching calls and interviews of various physical therapists, athletes, and coaches I've conducted. I always enjoy connecting with fellow triathletes. Feel free to contact me at Lance@LanceCarterCoaching.com.

You can receive the bonuses at
LanceCarterCoaching.com/LEARN

Testimonials

Lance coaches athletes in person and through his website LanceCarterCoaching.com. Here are a few testimonials from some of the thousands of athletes he has coached.

"Lance is one of the best coaches I've had, hands down! Not only is he patient, encouraging, and optimistic, but if I don't understand something explained one way, he has two or three different ways to explain it until I get the concept or idea that he's trying to teach. Some people can train to be a better coach. Lance is a natural." – Jannelle Cruz

"Lance, your coaching and mentorship is only eclipsed by your character and awesome personality. It was an honor to have you as our guide for this journey. Look forward to the next one!" – Jason Lukasek

"Lance has the gift of detecting and pulling potential out of a person. He found that I have an amazing ability to run which I never knew existed. He has given me strength to pursue this newfound ability with his invaluable coaching skills. Most important of all, I trust him. He makes my long term health a priority in all of my training plans." – Jamie Harris

"Lance's coaching helped me realize the athlete I could be. I came to him worried about finishing my first

race. With his coached practices and training plan, I was not only able to finish, but also place in my age group." Nathan Driggers

"Lance is an accomplished triathlete who uses compassion, training expertise, and enthusiasm to help people succeed. He has helped me find the inner confidence, drive, and discipline to achieve fitness and racing goals that I didn't think were possible." – Kelly Fisher

"My running has improved so much over the last 3 months. My form is stronger and more stable, and I'm running faster and more confidently. Lance is a solid coach that I've recommended to all my running friends who want to improve." - Rod Chavez

"Lance is such an outstanding coach because he clearly finds joy in helping people reach their goals - and he's good at it! Working with Lance has made me a faster, healthier, and happier runner after years of running the same pace. The cues he's provided on running form have been incredibly helpful, taking a solid 30 seconds off my mile pace. I love that he worked to figure out what cues resonated for me, rather than just giving generic advice." – Sarah Doherty

"After struggling just to finish my first half-Ironman, I decided to go with Lance as my coach for this year's

race. Not only did I feel much stronger in each aspect of my race, but I beat last year's time by 45 minutes. Lance is a great coach who knows how to get the best out of you and make training fun at the same time. Thanks Lance!" – Kris Vosk

"Lance is the best coach I've ever had. He knows more than anyone I've ever met about the details of training; how to get to the goal, how not to get injured in the process, how to design a plan that fits each individual. He is constantly gathering the latest information and evaluating what he feels works best for each athlete. Even more than being a wealth of knowledge though, his attitude is what helped me believe that I could do an Ironman. With him, I went from totally inexperienced triathlete to winning my age group at Cozumel and qualifying for Hawaii." - Kathryn Boddy

Citations

Vance, Jim, "The #1 Rule of Endurance Training"
home.trainingpeaks.com/blog/article/the-1-rule-of-
endurance-training

Scott, Dave, "Do what you can do in the moment."
DaveScottInc.com

About the *Six-Word Lessons Series*

Legend has it that Ernest Hemingway was challenged to write a story using only six words. He responded with the story, "For sale: baby shoes, never worn." The story tickles the imagination. Why were the shoes never worn? The answers are left up to the reader's imagination.

This style of writing has a number of aliases: postcard fiction, flash fiction, and micro fiction. Lonnie Pacelli was introduced to this concept in 2009 by a friend, and started thinking about how this extreme brevity could apply to today's communication culture of text messages, tweets and Facebook posts. He wrote the first book, *Six-Word Lessons for Project Managers*, then started helping other authors write and publish their own books in the series.

The books all have six-word chapters with six-word lesson titles, each followed by a one-page description. They can be written by entrepreneurs who want to promote their businesses, or anyone with a message to share.

See the entire *Six-Word Lessons Series* at 6wordlessons.com

Made in the USA
San Bernardino, CA
24 July 2016